Preparing for Dating and Marriage

Preparing for Dating and Marriage

A 31-DAY FAMILY DEVOTIONAL

CORY GRIESS

REFORMED
FREE PUBLISHING
ASSOCIATION
Jenison, Michigan

Reformed Free Publishing Association
1894 Georgetown Center Drive
Jenison MI 49428
616-457-5970
www.rfpa.org
mail@rfpa.org

Cover design by Amy Zevenbergen
Interior design by Katherine Lloyd / theDESKonline.com

ISBN: 978-1-944555-71-9
ISBN: 978-1-9444555-72-6 (ebook)
LCCN: 2020941906

With love and gratitude, I dedicate this book to my wife who helped me in the writing of the book (as she does in all things). Together with her, I also dedicate the book to the children the Lord has loaned to us. Children, it is our prayer that your marriages glorify your God and grant you a holy joy. We love you very much.

Contents

Principles to Undergird Your Search

Beware of Dangers

A Mysterious Joy

An Example to Emulate

Preface

When I was in high school I worked for my uncle doing drywall. Although it was good to be with my uncle, it wasn't my favorite job from my youth. I did learn some useful lessons though. There is even one I learned later looking back on those days: parenting is a lot like putting drywall mud on a wall. You have a little bit of time to mold and manipulate the material and then when the time is up that opportunity is over, never to return. God-fearing parents realize instinctively what little time they have to "train up a child in the way he should go" that "when he is old, he will not depart from it" (Prov. 22:6). But being reminded of it can encourage us to remain zealously active in the lives of our children. And maybe the reminder will prevent us from rushing through family worship (devotions) more often than we should, or help prevent us from skipping it altogether.

Fulfilling our calling with our children, we are to teach them many things. We are to teach them biblical doctrine and a godly walk of life. We are to teach them that they are members of the covenant of grace and that the covenant bears on all their existence. We recognize that their whole future life, should God bless our labors, is built upon this foundation. They have many important decisions to make and we pray our instruction helps them decide wisely.

One of the most important decisions our children will make regards who they will marry. So much of their life is affected by this decision. And not only *their* life, but also the lives of their children and grandchildren. Even the future of the church is affected by this decision.

Given the fact that who they marry is such a serious matter, it is almost shocking that at times Christian parents delay teaching their children on this point until they find out their child has been dating someone. Some even then do not teach their children, assuming their youth have learned enough from other sources. Children certainly do learn things about who they should date and marry from other sources, like church, and, if we are privileged to have one, a Christian school. They know basically what kind of person they should marry and why. But just as it is important to teach youth about sound doctrine in the home as well as in the church and school, so it is important for *parents*, not only the school and church, to teach their youth about dating and marriage. In fact, training about dating and marriage belongs chiefly to the sphere of the home. And it is the responsibility of the home to teach on this point *before* the children start dating. We want them to learn biblical doctrine when they are youth so that when they grow up and are challenged they can stand firm. Don't we also want them to learn a biblical view of dating and marriage when they are youth for the same reason?

There is a void of material to help parents do this. There is not a void of material on dating and marriage itself, but there is a void of material that helps the *parents teach their children* about this important topic. In fact, I could find nothing like this when looking for such help for myself as a parent. The following is intended to be such a guide. Written in a daily family devotional format, this book is meant to be a *help*. It is not intended to replace parental guidance ("here, go to your room and read

Preface

this"). It is intended to *help the parents* give that guidance, and to encourage parents in the giving of it. It is intended for an audience seventh grade and up, although even younger children will benefit. It does assume both a father and a mother in the home. It could still be used by a single parent with profit, but I recognize it may be painful for those in this heart-wrenching situation.

Each daily reading begins with a passage of scripture for the parents and children to look up and read together before reading the content of the devotion. You will also notice that there are questions at the end of each day's reading. The intention of these questions is to encourage and guide family discussion interacting with the material from the scripture and the daily reading. This material could profitably be used as a Bible study guide for youth in a church setting as well, but my first hope is that parents use it in their homes during family worship (devotions). I wrote it with this use first in mind. It is fine if younger children are present at these devotions. They will pick up more than you think, and I will alert you if anything sensitive to younger ears comes up in the material. Another option could be to use it before bed with child(ren) who are around the intended age; that would work well too.

I know youth at the age for whom this devotional is intended can be hard to draw out sometimes. And I can't promise this will be a magic bullet. But my prayer is that it will *help,* and that you will experience fellowship with your youth even as you teach and train.

Remember, the drywall is setting!

What Marriage Is

———

Marriage is God-Ordained

Read Genesis 2:18-25

In order to know what something is we have to know where it came from. If you had never seen an Xbox before, it would help to know who made it, why it was made, and something of how the maker intended it to work. So too with marriage.

We learn these things about marriage in Genesis 2. In verse 24 God defines marriage (which is why it is the most quoted verse about marriage in the Bible). "Therefore shall a man leave his father and his mother, and shall cleave unto his wife: and they shall be one flesh." God calls marriage a one-flesh union between one man and one woman who have left their parents to cleave to each other for life. It is a union of two so that they live together, raise a family together, if God is pleased to give them children, and "do life" together the rest of their days.

When a man and a woman stand up in front of the church and the minister pronounces them husband and wife, they don't feel a bolt of electricity zap them, and there is no glow that surrounds them. In fact, they might not feel different at all when it's over. Nonetheless, there is a God-created bond between those two that was not there before. No matter how the husband or wife feels about the marriage for the rest of his or her life, that bond has been created by God, and remains until God takes one in that marriage home to heaven.

In the way of *leaving* father and mother and *cleaving* to one's husband or wife, this bond is *experienced*. Cleaving physically, emotionally, spiritually to one another as the two live in their God-ordained roles, the couple *experiences* what God has put there between them. It is intimate; it is friendship; it is communication, the sharing of a life in the bonds of peace. It is hard work because both members of the marriage are sinners, but it is wonderful! It reflects the life God has within himself as triune, and the life that Christ and the church share with each other. And though sin has affected it tremendously, by grace, Christians may experience it as a glorious gift from God.

God made marriage to be this one-flesh union. And just like no one has the right to tell Kevin Bachus (the inventor of the Xbox) what an Xbox is and isn't, so also no one has the right to tell God (the creator of marriage) what marriage is and isn't. Marriage is God's institution for all people and all times and all places. God made a bond between *your* mom and dad years ago. And one day, Lord willing, he will make it between you and a husband or wife too.

Questions/Discussion Points

1. Does marriage sound exciting or scary or both? *[Parents, talk to your children about the good gift of marriage in your personal experience.]*

Day 1: Marriage is God-Ordained

2. Marriage is *God's* creation. How is the world rebelling against God by *telling him* what his invention is and is not?

3. What do you think it is like to cleave to your spouse "physically, emotionally, and spiritually?"

Day 2

God Brings a Spouse

Read Genesis 2:18–25 (again)

Verse 22 says God "brought her unto the man." This is God creating marriage! It's only after this that God calls the woman not merely "the woman," or a "help meet for Adam," but Adam's *wife* (v. 24). God performed the first wedding ceremony, bringing his daughter Eve to a godly man, Adam, and giving her away to him. God still does this. As the Reformed form for marriage puts it, this passage is God's witness "that He doth yet as with His hand bring unto every man his wife."*

It is possible to marry the "wrong person," that is, marrying an unbeliever in disobedience to God's word. If you do, we as your parents may be responsible for that (along with you), and so with this devotional we are going to teach you to guard your heart. But once a marriage is made, then in God's sovereignty, even if it is to the "wrong person," it is in fact the "right person," the person you were supposed to marry. God brings to every man his wife. And God makes even sinful unions permanent.

---

* Form for the Confirmation of Marriage Before the Church, in *The Confessions and Church Order of the Protestant Reformed Churches* (Grandville, MI: Protestant Reformed Churches in America, 2005), 305–10.

Day 2: God Brings a Spouse

How does he bring to every man his wife and to every woman her husband today? Not the same way he did for Adam and Eve of course. He does so by his providence. As he leads us to seek the right kind of spouse, and as we learn the teaching of his word regarding what marriage is, the goal of marriage, what to look for in a spouse, principles to follow in looking for a spouse, dangers to avoid, and examples to follow—he providentially leads us to our "Adam" or our "Eve." That list above is everything we will discuss in the next twenty-nine days.

The process we carry out when seeking a spouse is commonly called dating. But no matter what you call it, dating, courtship, or something else, it is a process spoken of in Genesis 2:24. It is the process of leaving father and mother and cleaving to a wife (or husband). The key is that we learn this process from the word and not the world. May God grant his grace as we learn from his word in this study and may he in time and by his providence bring a godly wife or husband by his hand for you.

Questions/Discussion Points

1. Maybe you haven't thought about dating yet. Maybe right now you don't even desire it. Nevertheless, why is it important to learn what God's word says about dating and marriage *before* you get married or even begin dating? Maybe you *are* dating or desire to date. Why is it still important to go through this material now?

2. How can we pray today for your future marriage? *[Fathers, please close devotions by praying for the potential future spouses and marriages of your children.]*

The Goals of Dating and Marriage

To Glorify God

Read Ephesians 5:22–33

This is a new section, the *goals* of dating and marriage. There are five of these goals. The first one, though, is first for a reason. There is a great temptation to view marriage (and therefore dating) as all about you. It isn't. It's first about God. It was created by God as a good gift for you that is for sure. But, more than that, it was created for his own glory. And ironically, unless we view it that way, we won't have the joy that comes with it. Our benefit always comes to us through the "back door." When we try to make our benefit come through the "front door" by seeking ourselves first, we lose it as a benefit altogether.

Before you start thinking about what you want in a spouse and hoping God's will conforms to your desires, your greatest desires must be conformed to his will. What does God's child seek more than the glory of his Father? He wants his Father to be honored, respected, and adored. Your heavenly Father has redeemed you out of the house of the evil one into his own house. You must go into dating with "hallowed be Thy name" in your heart and on your lips. And when you do, you will go into marriage the same way.

How does marriage glorify God? Chiefly, in its display of his relationship in Jesus Christ to his church. Marriage is not the main thing; Jesus and his church are. Your marriage will be temporary. Earthly marriage will eventually give way to the eternal reality of Christ's marriage to his church. That glorious end is what our marriage now is supposed to point to.

Marriage is a means to magnify the bond between God and his people. It does so by the husband leading his wife in love like Christ does. It does so by the wife submitting to her husband in humility and devotion, like the church does (imperfectly). Marriage magnifies the bond between God and his people by husband and wife embracing each other in selfless love patterned after Christ and his bride. It's tempting for us parents to forget to start here when teaching about dating and marriage. We so desperately want you to marry the right kind of person for *your benefit* and the benefit of our grandchildren. But we have to remember to point you here. Marry someone committed to living like Christ and his church, not just because it will give you a good marriage, but because it will put on display the glory of your beloved God.

Questions/Discussion Points

1. Imagine your spouse was in an accident and was paralyzed. His/her looks were marred. You couldn't talk with him/her or have children. Your role would be to serve him/her and receive very little earthly benefit in return. What would be the only motive for staying in that marriage as God calls you to do? Would God bless you in it also?

2. Can you think of other ways (besides picturing Christ and the church) marriage glorifies God?

Day 4

To Raise
a Godly Seed

Read Malachi 2:11–16

Why did God make marriage? And what should your goal be in pursuing it? We have given one answer so far, the glory of God. A second goal is so that there might be "a godly seed" (v. 15). Malachi's prophesy here is an accusing one. He admonishes the returned captives for sins in marriage and family. A good number of Israelite men were forsaking their godly Israelite wives for younger pagan women (vv. 11, 14). The damage being done to the wives and the children, God says, is emotional and spiritual *treachery* and *violence*.

As God charges the Israelite men for their sin, he reminds them of one of the main purposes for giving them their godly Israelite wives in the first place, "that he might seek a godly seed." God created marriage for his people to raise up the next generation in godliness and faithfulness.

This was one of the main purposes for making two become one in the beginning. In fact, the first thing God mentions to Adam and Eve after creating them male and female in his image is, "Be fruitful and multiply, and replenish the earth" (Gen. 1:28).

Day 4: To Raise a Godly Seed

The earth was to be filled from shore to shore with sons and daughters who would glorify God in their lives, using the earth to magnify him.

We have to consider this as part of our goal in getting married. Can I raise godly children with this person? Can this person raise godly children with me? It's hard sometimes to think that far down the road, but when you date, we your parents are going to discuss this with you openly. What will it be like when you have children to raise? Picture her as a mother someday. Picture him as a father someday. Will you be unified in your purpose with your children? Do you share the same convictions about what your home life will be like, what your priorities will be? Will you be able to help each other grow in parenting?

God does not give children to every marriage, and it is painful when that is the case. Or sometimes there are ungodly children who grow up in godly homes. If either is the case in your future, you will still find many joys in your life and opportunities to serve God that you hadn't considered before. But most often God gives children to a couple and gives them the joy and struggle to raise them together, so that blessed by him, another generation may rise up faithful to him on the earth.

Questions/Discussion Points

1. What would it be like if your dad and mom had very different convictions about how to raise children? Some hypotheticals to consider could be: priorities, goals, entertainment, nurture, discipline, Sabbath observance, schooling, etc.

2. In the passage we read today is there a connection between God's hatred of divorce (v. 16) and his seeking a godly seed (v. 15)? How does that affect what you look for in a spouse?

To Promote the Health of the Church

Read Psalm 128

The future of the church will be wrapped up in your marriage. Weak marriages generally make for weak homes. Weak homes generally make for a weak church. Psalm 128 describes a godly marriage and a godly home. The Psalm begins by saying the one who fears the Lord is blessed. It then goes on in verses 2-4 to describe that blessedness in the man's family life. And then in verses 5-6 the Psalm says that this man shall "see the good of Jerusalem [the church] all the days of [his] life," and in the generations following, "peace upon Israel." One of the connections here is that the godly family of this man who fears the Lord, is part of the way in which there is good in Jerusalem.

This sounds weird at first, but one of the goals of marriage ought to be the good of the church, present and future. A strong, godly, unified marriage is a good example to others in the church. A good strong marriage often produces good strong youth for the church. A faithful marriage even means less time working on your own marriage problems so that there is more time for the couple and family together to serve others in and out of the church.

But there is a reciprocal relationship here too. Verse 5 also says that the man who fears the Lord *is blessed out of Zion*. That is, his marriage and his family receive blessing from their life in the church. This is so true also. There are examples of other godly marriages around you to help when yours is difficult. The accountability, the friendship, the fellowship, the word preached and studied, all of it will help your marriage and family. Live your life in the church and your marriage will be strengthened by it.

Marry with this goal in mind then: that you live in the church with your spouse and family, so that the church may bless you, and so that you and your marriage and children may bless the church.

Questions/Discussion Points

1. Maybe you are thinking, "Come on! Dating and marriage are only supposed to be about the feelings and the romance, right? Isn't it a little hyper-spiritual to be thinking about the church (especially generations from now) in dating and marriage?" But why should the health of the church be so important to us when we date and marry?

2. How is living "out of Zion" a blessing to our family?

Day 6

———

To Provide for
the Woman's Security

Read Ruth 3:1-2

It is not the case that a person never thinks about himself/herself when considering dating and marriage. Absolutely not! Marriage is a good gift from God to his people, and one of the goals of marriage is to prayerfully seek this good gift for oneself. Wonderfully though, if one is seeking the first three goals we've studied already (God's glory, a godly seed, and the welfare of the church) then generally one will be blessed with what one needs and enjoys from marriage. For a woman, that is especially the *security* we discuss today. For a man it is especially the *respect* we will discuss tomorrow.

You know the history of Ruth. We are going to come back to this history at the end of this devotional, but for now, remember she was a Moabitess convert who returned with Naomi to the promised land and the covenant people of God. Naomi was getting older, and Ruth was not getting younger. Naomi could have assumed Ruth would take care of her the rest of her life, but she knew the best thing for Ruth would be that Ruth get married. In Ruth 3:1 Naomi describes the benefit she seeks for Ruth in marriage, "My daughter, shall I not seek rest for thee?" The word "rest" could also be translated, "peace," "welfare," "joy," but especially, "*security*." Naomi wanted Ruth to have the "rest" of "security" that a godly marriage can bring. A woman needs security, and when she has it, she thrives.

That security is threefold. First, there is *physical* security. A godly man will provide what his wife and family physically need the best he is able. There is a sense of being settled, at peace, secure in a faithful husband's providing that is important for a woman. Second, there is *emotional* security. A woman finds emotional security in the love of her husband. She does not worry that there are other loves in his life but may instead rest in the knowledge that he is committed to her. She does not have to bear the burdens of life alone, she is emotionally protected and cared for by her godly husband. Third, a God-fearing marriage provides *spiritual* security to a woman of God. There is a "rest" in the knowledge that her husband will lead her in God's ways also with her help. There is a security to be found in trusting that he will lead the family in the fear of the Lord both in doctrine and in life. There is a peace in being confident that he will grow in the strength and knowledge of Jehovah to apply God's word to her and the children and their life together as a family.

Naomi sought this for Ruth. As your parents, we desire this for our daughters and seek to teach our sons to provide it for a woman someday. It is not selfish to want this for yourself, and it is not selfish for your parents to seek it for you. God says this is one of the purposes of marriage. We are your parents, and we love our daughter like Naomi loved Ruth. How could we not seek rest for you?

Questions/Discussion Points

1. Some people teach that a biblical marriage is not security but a prison for a woman. There are marriages that *are* prisons for a woman. But can you explain why many think even a *biblical* marriage is a prison and why they're wrong?

2. *[For daughters]* In what ways do you see the need for this threefold security in a godly marriage someday?

3. Give specific examples of how a man, before marriage, demonstrates that he will be able to provide physical, emotional, and spiritual security.

To Encourage the Man's Confident Service

Read Ephesians 5:23-33

We already read this passage back on day three, and we will read it again later. Ephesians 5 is the great portion of scripture on marriage and the calling of a husband and wife. Interestingly, in this passage, when the apostle speaks of the calling of the wife, he never says that she is to love her husband. What makes this more striking is that the apostle *does* repeatedly call the *husband* to love his wife. While a wife must love her husband too, that isn't the main thing the apostle focuses on when he speaks of the wife's relationship to her husband. Instead, he focuses on "reverence," that is, *respect*, or *honor*. Verse 33 says, "Nevertheless let every one of you in particular so love his wife even as himself; and the wife see that she reverence her husband." A man needs respect or honor from his wife.

To respect or honor someone is to acknowledge the person's position given by God. Respect includes showing thankfulness, submission, and faithfulness to someone. Respect will take the word and judgment of someone as weighty. Ideally then, respect includes thinking highly of the person. The opposite of respect would be behavior that is uncharitable toward someone or that seeks to undermine their position, going against them, whether bluntly or subtly.

A man must be respect*able* of course. But a man cannot fulfill his callings very well if his wife does not respect him, sinner though he is. When a man knows his wife respects him, honors him, and appreciates him in spite of his sins and shortcomings, that man is spurred on to be the leader in his home. He goes to work with confidence and joy. He works in the church with a support that is encouraging. It is a great responsibility to be head of a home, to provide security for a wife and family. The man who knows his wife respects him for his efforts is spurred on to more growth and faithfulness. Without this, the man languishes. He is tempted to give up. He finds no joy in his callings. Son, it is not selfish to seek to marry a woman who respects you. God himself says this is one of his purposes for marriage.

Do you see how God made the marriage relationship to fit together? A woman needs love and security, and when her husband gives it, she has a strong respect for him. Likewise, when a woman has a strong respect for her husband, he is spurred on to love and protect her physically, emotionally, and spiritually. Picture it like a bicycle. You push down on one pedal and the other comes up—push on the other and the previous one comes up. God's design is wonderful!

Questions/Discussion Points

1. *[For sons]* In what ways do you see that having this kind of respect from your wife someday would help you with your callings? Conversely, how would marrying a woman who does not respect you make for misery?

2. What kind of man is respect*able*?

3. What are some specific ways that a woman, before marriage, demonstrates that she will respect and honor her husband?

Whom to Look for
and Who to Be

Day 8

———

Filial Fear

Read Psalm 19:14

This new section is about whom to look for and who to be as you seek the kind of marriage God created, and as you seek the goals for marriage we have described. First, you must look for a Christian, for you are a Christian. The Canons of Dordt in the first head of doctrine, article 12 describes the fruits of election in a child of God. One of those fruits is "filial fear." Filial means childlike. Fear means awe and reverence. But when we put filial together with fear something wonderful is added to fear. It's still awe and reverence, but it's mixed with a deep love that gives one a desire to please. It's the attitude of heart found in the Psalmist at the end of Psalm 19, "Let the words of my mouth, and the meditation of my heart, be acceptable in thy sight, O LORD, my strength, and my redeemer." Here is a petition that if truly prayed, only comes from a child of God.

From the words of your mouth, to the things you spend time thinking about, to the works of your hands, do you not want to please him ("acceptable in thy sight")? We know that you, and we too, fall so far short of what we desire. But we are growing! We live every moment before his face. He sees all our thoughts, actions, and words ("in Thy sight"). Self-seeking stains everything we put our mind, mouth, and movements to. Nonetheless, he sees the battle we are engaged in against our old man, and is himself the origin of it. And in fighting that battle out of love and respect for him, the child of God in Christ can and does please his Father, walking in his ways (Ps. 147:11; 1 Thess. 4:1, etc.).

Who is our Heavenly Father, to draw out such a cry from his children as is found in Psalm 19:14? He is a Father so great and so good and so faithful to his children! He is the Father who has adopted us into his own family out of the family of the evil one, and has done it with no assistance from anyone, certainly not his children. He is a Father who provides, who keeps his word, who never wavers from his commitment of love and protection. He gives a future and a hope to his children that is unwavering and truly good. He is the Lord, Jehovah, the Father who in covenant love causes his life to flow in and through his children as any good father should.

A kind of heart that prays Psalm 19:14's prayer is what you look for first, and this kind of heart we pray is developing in you for the sake of your spouse. This is why we as your parents have structured your life the way we have. Full of biblical instruction, church, school, and a family life centered on the word. We want you to grow as a child who knows in truth, loves, and wants to please our Father in gratitude for his redeeming grace.

No idealism of course. It's always a small beginning of the new obedience. And there remains in the best of us the great infirmity of self-love to wrestle with all our life long. That will be your spouse, and it will be you too. But, seeing sin for what it is, and humbled by it, continually taking refuge in the blood, death, and obedience of our Lord Jesus Christ, you and your spouse must be people who can say together: "In every aspect of our lives, we want to please our Father." In this case, "brothers" and "sisters" can marry.

Questions/Discussion Points

1. Look up the two verses referenced in today's devotional about pleasing God (Ps. 147:11; 1 Thess. 4:1). Do you want to please God? Why? How *can* sinners please God?

2. In what ways would we find evidence that someone you want to date wants to please God? What kinds of questions will you/we ask, and what will we observe?

———

A Man Submitted to King Jesus

Read 1 Corinthians 11:3

For the next four days we are going to answer the question whom must you *look for* (if you are a *girl* looking for a godly *boy*); and who must you *be* (if you are a *boy* seeking to be a godly husband for a godly *girl* someday). We'll switch it around the next four days after that.

If you are going to seek a godly man for a husband someday, daughter, you are going to be looking for a man willing to be very different from the men of the world. If you are going to be a godly man for a wife someday, son, you must be maturing into a man very different from the men of the world. The heart of that difference will be in a man's recognition that he is under the headship of King Jesus.

God is head of Christ—in his humanity Christ submits to God. Christ is head of his church and therefore is head over every man in his church. Similarly, the husband is the head of his wife, "And the head of the woman is the man." Christ is head over every woman in his church too, to be sure. And every woman must disobey her husband if he leads her to go against her first head, Christ. But in God's arrangement of things, though man and woman are equally cherished image bearers before God, the husband is head of his wife in the home.

This means real authority. But authority, under authority. The husband's rule over his wife and home is constantly under surveillance. He must assert *Christ's* rule over his home, and in *Christ's* way. What a responsibility! *God* places this weight upon him, and will require it of him!

But think about the wife too! What a thing for a woman to do, to marry a man and give herself to his headship! What a risk! She swears an oath to be subject to her husband's headship until death! She can't do it unless she is as confident as she can be in this life that this man will live in his role as her head and the head of her children, with one eye always upon his own head Jesus Christ.

There are two temptations men face when they become head of their home. Usually a man is tempted by one or the other, though some are tempted by both in different ways. The one temptation is to become a dictator with the position as head. The other is to be lazy, giving up the position to his wife. The only defense is a spiritual one, and it defends against both temptations. We read in 1 Corinthians 11:3, "The head of every man is Christ." The man who lives before the face of Christ, cannot but work against his lazy nature to take up the position Christ gives him, the best he is able. The man who lives before the face of Christ, will fight against his old man so that he uses his position for the sake of the well-being of his family and not for selfish ends. Daughter, seek a man who in doctrine and life, makes much of Christ! Oh Lord, grow our son to be such a man!

Day 9: A Man Submitted to King Jesus

1. How can you tell if a man lives daily under the headship of King Jesus?

2. How does a young man's respect for his parents and/or church officebearers reveal this?

3. *[For sons]* How is the world trying to get you to rebel against your head? In what ways are you tempted?

A Man Who Will Sacrifice for His Wife

Read Ephesians 5:22–27

I know, this is the third time we've read this. You're going to have this passage memorized by the time we are finished! But the more we read something the more we notice things in what we read. Notice *where* Ephesians 5:25 is found in the chapter. It is right *after* the call for headship in verses 23–24. The Spirit is saying by this arrangement, "Take up your headship, but remember to use it in love for your bride!" Verse 25 is also right *before* the call to seek the holiness of one's wife in verses 26–27. The Spirit is saying, "This is the approach you take toward growing her in holiness, set it in the context of sacrificial love for her."

So the call is not for sacrificial love for her totally apart from caring about her growth in godliness. Neither is it a call to care about her growth in godliness in a distant, cold, manner. It's, "Husbands, *love* your wives, even as Christ also loved the church, and gave himself for it; *That* he might sanctify and cleanse it with the washing of water by the word, *That* he might present it to himself a glorious church, not having spot, or wrinkle, or any such thing; but that it should be holy and without blemish" (vv. 25–27, italics mine). A husband's sacrificial love is, generally speaking, a power the Spirit uses for the holiness of a wife! She knows Christ's sacrificial love better having known that of her husband. She is impelled toward holiness by it.

From a biblical point of view, the proof of love is a willingness to give of oneself for the sake of the other. That is how God showed his love. Giving of oneself is a litmus test for love in all relationships, and no less in marriage. Strong emotions make it easier to give oneself for another, (which is not a bad thing of course!) but the real test comes when emotions are not as strong. That is why the advice has often been, "Daughter(s), don't look so much at how he treats *you*, but at how he treats his sister(s) and his mother and his friends he has known for a long time. There you will see how he really loves for the long haul."

Son(s), do you want to grow to be a godly husband to a godly wife someday? Then love your sister(s), your mother, and your friends, with sacrificial care. Help them grow in godliness, give them a good example, and make them want to follow it by the way you are willing to give yourself selflessly for their well-being.

And do it because Christ has done just that, and is doing just that, for you. He gave himself for you first, before he ever called you to holiness. He gives himself for you now, interceding for you and advocating for you every day, even while he calls you to holiness. He gave and gives himself, *that* we might be sanctified and cleansed.

Questions/Discussion Points

1. *[For sons]* If you wanted to date a girl and she asked herself, "How does he treat his sister(s) and his mother," what would her answer be?

2. What does it look like when a man gives himself sacrificially for a woman?

A Man Who Nurtures Godliness

Read Ephesians 5:25–30

Remember we are thinking about what kind of boy a *girl* should *look for*, and what kind of boy a *young man* should strive *to be*.

The goal of a husband's headship and love for his wife and children is the same as Christ's goal with his headship and love of his church. In Ephesians 5:26 we read, "That he might sanctify and cleanse [her] with the washing of water by the word." A husband's ultimate goal with his headship is the holiness of his family. In verse 29, this part of his leadership and love is called nourishing and cherishing.

To nourish means "to care for the growth of with great care." To cherish means "to tenderly care for." Both words call to mind the image of a gardener and his flowers. He nurtures them and tenderly cares for them so that they develop, grow, and blossom. He cannot be rough with them or they crack and break. He cannot be neglectful either, or they wilt. He has to supply what is needed regularly—food, water, sunshine. Carefully and wisely, he has to pull up weeds and prune the branches. And as he does that, the flower matures and blooms for all to see.

So too the husband and father. His love for his family is that he nourishes and cares for his wife and children unto a blooming godliness. He cannot be too rough with them or they break emotionally. He must give what is needed for mind, body, and soul. He gives the food of encouragement and instruction from the word. He gives the water of time well spent and the sunshine of his example. He pulls weeds of sin and prunes ungodly patterns carefully. He knows when a rebuke is needed, and he gives it carefully. He knows when encouragement is needed, and he gives that freely. Under his nurture and tender care, the wife and children, by grace, bloom with spirituality and a humble confidence born of their surety that they are redeemed by King Jesus.

Daughter, this is a spiritual "art" that needs to be there in bud form in the man you marry. Son, this is a spiritual art that needs to be there in bud form in you for the sake of the woman you marry.

Questions/Discussion Points

1. *[For sons]* As a husband, do you think you would be more tempted to be harsh, or more tempted to be passive, too hesitant to "prune" your family?

2. *[For daughters]* Why is it important that your husband be able to first, gently care for you, and second, wisely stand up to you if need be?

Day 12

A Man of the Word

Read Ephesians 5:26–27

In order for a man to lead his wife and home in godliness, he must be growing as a man of the word. Christ seeks the godliness of his bride by the means of the word. Ephesians 5:26 tells us, "That he might sanctify and cleanse it with the washing of water *by the word*" (emphasis added). The word not only declares to God's people that they are not guilty of their sin, but it is also a bucket of soapy water in the hands of the Spirit to cleanse them from that sin.

A husband is to take up the word in his home. He is himself part of the bride which Christ washes by the word. He is himself being made holy as the word conforms him to the image of Christ. As one who has benefited from the word, he uses the word in his home. As Christ really *serves* his bride by taking up the word and cleansing her with it, so must a godly husband *serve* his wife and family.

That certainly means bringing his family to a faithful true church to come under the washing of the word in the proclamation of it. As the Israelite fathers led their families back from Babylon and to the faithful means of grace, so a godly husband and father will lead his home to the faithful means of grace in the church. (Ezra 2 lists the returnees by families under the names of the *fathers*). The faithful husband and father says to his family, "Let us go into the house of the LORD!" (Ps. 122:1). If he is unfaithful in seeking the means of grace, he cannot faithfully lead a wife and family.

A godly husband will study the word himself. He will study it in Bible study, in small group discussions, and in his own personal devotional life. He will do this not only for himself, but also for the sake of being able to serve his family with the word; so that he is able to apply the word to his wife and children and to direct his home in godliness. There are times when the wife is more *capable* spiritually than the husband, and that is fine. But it ought never be the case that a man sits back and says, "She is the spiritual one, not me. I will just earn the paycheck; she will take care of the rest." Daughter, don't marry a man like that. Son, don't become that man.

Questions/Discussion Points

1. After you get out of high school, there is a great drop-off in other people serving the word to you. You become more responsible for ingesting the word for yourself. How can we prepare for that now?

2. *[Fathers, perhaps you could use this opportunity to share with your son(s) challenges you have faced in learning to lead your own family with the word.]*

3. From a review of Days 9–12, what does it mean to "be a man," and how is that different from what the world terms, "being a man?"

Day 13

———

A Woman with a Submitted Heart

Read Ephesians 5:22–24 (now from the other perspective)

For the next four days we are meditating on what kind of girl a *young man* should *look for*, and what kind of girl a *young woman* should strive *to be*.

Girls, if you are going to be a godly wife for a godly man one day, you are going to have to be different from most women in our culture. Boys, if you are going to be a man who seeks a godly wife, you are going to seek a woman who is different from most women in our culture. That difference will start in a woman's heart and work its way out from there. In her heart and her life, she will be growing in, and desiring to be growing in, *submission*.

Uh-oh. The "s" word. You knew it would be coming! But actually it has already come. It was used of the godly man on Day 9 who is called to *submit* to King Jesus in his role as head. We are *all* called to submit. It's just a question of when, where, and how. The difference is that a wife's *role* in her marriage is fulfilled in submission to her husband (Eph 5:22, 24; Col. 3:18; Titus 2:4; 1 Pet. 3:1).

The call of the scriptures here is to three things. First, it is a call to a humble attitude of the heart. The very word the scriptures use for submission in Ephesians 5 indicates a willingness of the heart. So, submission to a husband begins with submission to God in Christ. If Christ says, "submit to your husband," the young woman is looking forward to submitting to her husband as unto her Lord, knowing it is good, right, and the best thing for her, for she trusts her Christ. This kind of heart allows submission in *attitude* even when a husband is wrong and she must say something as his wife (which she must!). "I know you are my husband and I respect your God-given position. If this is still your position after we talk, I will abide by it. It's not sinful, and I am your wife and am under your headship. But I don't think this is wise and I want to help you. I think I have a perspective on this that might change your approach."

Second, the call to submission really is a call to flat-out obedience (Titus 2:4). Doesn't the church *obey* Christ her head? So too a God-fearing wife in everything lawful. If her husband abuses that call of God upon her life, she goes to the elders of the church—she runs there!—with not one shred of guilt. But a wife is called by God to obey her husband.

Third, the call to submission is a call for a wife to use all her gifts, abilities, wisdom, and creativity, to hold her husband high, to help him be honorable in the callings God has given him. The church seeks to magnify Christ. A wife seeks to magnify her husband, especially in her helping him to be the man he is called to be in church, home, and society. She knows she has gifts, abilities, intelligence, perhaps a perspective different from his. She may offer a corrective to his weaknesses. She may offer insight where he is blind. His heart trusts in her. He ought to be able to carry out his callings before God fifty times better because of the good gift his wife is to him. Among the other things a wife may and does do, she ought to find her greatest fulfillment in this.

Daughter, may God grow you into this kind of woman. Son, pursue her, and God give you to find her.

Questions/Discussion Points

1. How could Christ's calling to submit to a husband be good for a Christian wife?

2. How can a young woman grow in this submission before she gets married?

3. *[For sons]* Given today's meditation, why would it be good to get to know your girlfriend's mother?

Day 14

A Woman Who Has God's Goals for Her Family Life

Read Titus 2:4–5

A godly woman will be "swimming upstream" with respect to the goals of her life, especially in the desire to be a "keeper at home."

Ordered rightly, the Christian home is a foretaste of heaven. In Psalm 23 David calls heaven the "house of the LORD." The Lord spoke of heaven as "Father's house [of] many mansions" (John 14:2). The home we live in ought to be a tiny taste of Father's house. William Cowper once said, "Domestic happiness! Thou only bliss of Paradise that hast survived the fall!"[*] It's not *totally* true. He was forgetting about the church. Nonetheless, the Christian home is one of the few places that exist where heavenly shelter from the way of the world is known.

To be such, the Christian home must be a place of refuge from the godlessness of the age, a place where one can shut the door on the world and find the peace of God's covenant life. The Christian home must be a place where life's difficulties are

---

[*] Quoted in B. M. Palmer and J. W. Alexander, *The Family* (Harrisonburg, VA: Sprinkle Publications, 1981) 179.

downloaded in conversation and then uploaded in prayer. The Christian home is a place where in songs sung, prayers prayed, discipline conducted, and encouragement given, we grow up together in Christ. A Christian home must be a place of fellowship, where the aroma of the care of Christ Jesus spreads to every corner. This is truly a taste of heaven in this world!

The God-fearing wife and mother is the keeper of this place! The word "keeper" means a watch, sentinel, guardian, protector. She is queen of the family, and the home is her castle. She works tirelessly to make a house into a home and to keep it that way. It's never heaven, there's always but a *taste* of it there. But under her husband's kingship this is her calling and her life. What a high and noble calling to be a home-maker! A home is not automatic, she makes a home! This is no job left to the weak and frail. Should you dare to pursue creating a place that reflects heaven itself on earth? This takes a tremendous amount of wisdom, intelligence, skill, grace, godliness, and hard work. Most of all it takes a God-fearing woman's wholehearted commitment to love her God and her husband and her children out of the grace shown to her (Titus 2:4). And since love is a supernatural power, it takes heaven in her to do it.

Girls, it goes against the grain to give your life to this. But be sure it went against the grain in Paul's and Titus' time too. Paul speaks of men "who subvert whole houses, teaching things which they ought not" (Titus 1:11). In a world of subverted, upside-down homes, may God give you the joy of keeping one right-side up.

Questions/Discussion Points

1. Name and explain specific things a God-fearing woman does to make her home a taste of heaven?

2. How does Satan use the world to make this goal look worthless? How does he make it seem like this goal is only for a foolish, simple, backward woman?

A Woman Who
is No Brawler

Read Proverbs 21:9

Remember we are studying what to look for and who to be, now
from the perspective of what kind of woman to look for, and what
kind of woman by grace to strive to be. Don't look for, and may
God keep you from growing into, a woman who is a *brawler*. A
brawling woman is a woman who always stirs up strife and con-
tention with her husband. She is very quick with a sharp word,
ready to say something to get under her husband's skin, to jab at
him, to cut him down, to find fault. She is quick to start an argu-
ment. He comes home from work and she has been harboring
something up from that morning, mulling it over all day. Now,
she unleashes it upon him and does not stop. She nags and nags.
Proverbs 19:13 speaks of her as a continual dropping, or drip-
ping, of rain. There is a form of torture where a regular drip of
water falling on a bound victim's head drives the person insane.
So a man caught in a marriage to a brawling woman whom he
cannot (may not) escape. He is subject to a torture of the soul.

Though the man may not escape, he does his best to avoid his
wife, at least when she is at her worst. He gives up the rest of his

wide house to live in a corner on the housetop, where even bad weather is preferable to being close to her. And, though he cannot and may not, he thinks about how much better it would be to live alone out in the wilderness, than with her (21:19). There is a "scale" of brawling women, from the woman who occasionally nags to the extreme example given in Proverbs. Nevertheless, there are men for whom even this extreme example is all too real.

Sometimes it is the man's fault, or at least partly so. He fails so obviously and willingly and unrepentantly in his role as husband that he drives his hurt wife to bitterness (in which case she must bring him to the elders instead of brawl). But there are cases too, where the woman had brawling as the example in her mother, and other cases where deep down a woman harbors a desire to be with a previous boyfriend whom she regrets got away. In the end, though, there is a desire for control in all cases, and unwillingness to be content with God's way.

This woman is the opposite of everything discussed so far. She does not have a submissive heart. She doesn't have as her goal to provide a home that is a foretaste of heaven, or has long ago given up the thought. The one who ought to be "a crown to her husband," becomes instead, "rottenness in his bones" (Prov. 12:4). She is bone of his bone and flesh of his flesh, but her contribution rots him from within. Some men, by their sinful pursuits of lust in young years end up "stuck" in this situation for the rest of their lives.

Seek God's way and his way alone. If you end up in this situation, bringing one's wife to the elders, along with an even more fervent sacrificial love, is the path to follow.

May no daughter of this house end up becoming this woman. A humble heart that knows sin and grace, and walks before Jehovah's face in contented service to him will prevent it.

Day 15: A Woman Who is No Brawler

As a sunflower orients itself every moment of the day to the sun, so the contented woman orients herself to God's will for her life and lives as he calls her to live.

Questions/Discussion Points

1. Do you think we (as the bride of Christ) are ever a brawling wife to Christ? Think of our complaining!

2. *[Read Hebrews 12:15 together.]* How is bitterness like a root that springs up?

3. What is the difference between a wife's nagging/ brawling, and her humble and careful correcting of her husband?

A Woman of Modesty

Read 1 Timothy 2:9–10

The biblical word for modesty has as a root meaning "to order or arrange appropriately." Ordering the heart right by grace, a woman will order her outward appearance right too. Just as the mouth speaks what is the overflow of the heart, so the outward adornment reveals something about the clothing on the heart. Adorning oneself with modest clothes is on the outside. But the apostle says, the God-fearing woman is to do that, "with shamefacedness and sobriety" both of which are heart words.

Shamefacedness and sobriety are words referring to an inner recoiling from anything that is shameful to God. Shamefacedness and sobriety are the heart's blush at what is displeasing to our Father. The words also indicate a certain control of oneself to keep one's heart ordered aright. So that if the intrigue of enticement, or even merely the desire to make oneself the center of attention, is tempting, this woman has a governor on her heart to seek God above these things. She lives before his face and not the face of men (males). Her confidence is in God, not in what men are thinking of her.

This heart is something you can see in a woman. In conversation, in the way she handles herself, in her attitude, and in her seeking to serve others. It's not a specific personality trait. There may be women with big personalities who are still modest of heart. It's not seen in that a woman is somber and never laughs. Rather, shamefacedness and sobriety result in a desire to keep oneself submitted to Jehovah.

This heart is also something you can see in a woman's clothes. She is not disheveled and homely as possible as though that is modesty. But she is appropriate—lovely, well-ordered. She is not seeking attention by showing too much skin. She is not drawing focus upon herself by homeliness or extravagance. This is the apostles' point about broided hair, pearls, and costly array. In the world this represents anything to draw undue attention to oneself and to express one's pride and self-promotion by outward dress.

Daughter(s), this is why we teach you about true beauty from the inside to the outside, so that by God's grace working in you, you desire to order yourself outside according to a well-ordered heart inside. Sons, this is why we teach you to seek a woman who is ordered under the gaze of God in her heart, mind, attitude, and even her dress. Just as the mouth speaks what is the overflow of the heart, so the outward adornment reveals something about the clothing on the soul. What kind of woman do you want teaching your daughters about these things some day?

Questions/Discussion Points

1. What do you think is the motivation of someone who dresses immodestly?

2. What does dressing for God's glory in this culture look like in your opinion? Be as specific as possible.

Principles to Undergird Your Search

Be Not
Unequally Yoked

Read 2 Corinthians 6:14–18

We move now to some specific scriptural principles for dating to
help us on our way toward a faithful marriage (under the blessing of God). Hopefully, given everything that you know already,
and given what we have discussed so far in this devotional, you
could give some, if not all of these principles yourself. This first
one is the obvious one, but no less important: a believer may not
marry an unbeliever. And if you may not *marry* an unbeliever,
there is no reason to *date* him or her either.

Marriage is like a husband and wife "yoked" to a plow
together. How's that for romantic! But its true. They move as one,
as two animals yoked together move as one. If they want to go
different directions it doesn't work. One will eventually win and
be the stronger influence on the other. Because yoked, you see,
they *must* move in one direction.

Marriage is a *life-long* commitment to be yoked together.
But isn't *dating* a certain "yoked together" too? Dating is more
than a friendship. And even a friendship has a certain "yoked
together"-ness about it. If you are too close to an unbeliever in

friendship you quickly become too close to the world because you move along with that person to his/her goals and desires. How much more is this not true in dating? Dating is for marriage. It isn't marriage, but it is *for* marriage. You ought not look at dating as simply having a fling for fun. It is trying on the yoke in some limited ways to see if you can permanently tie the knot on that yoke, never to have it off again (until death). If you can't buy the car, what reason is there to tempt yourself by taking it out for a joy-ride?

The importance of recognizing this becomes clear when the text gives the reason why a believer and unbeliever may not be yoked together. There are two principles of life at work in a believer and an unbeliever, and they are as opposite as the principles of life in Christ and the devil. The principle of life in an unbeliever is death. An unregenerate person is alive physically but dead spiritually. It's the same principle in your old man, but it is all there is in an unbeliever. It's a principle of life that seeks to be God, rather than submit to God. It seeks to run away from God, not to him. The principle of life in you is indeed life. It battles the principle of death remaining. It wants to bow to Jehovah as Father and walk with him in every way in the path of life. It wants to run to him in repentance seeking forgiveness and restoring love even if you walked away for a season. If you hooked Christ and the devil up to a plow and said now plow together, it would be impossible. They don't have to try it to figure it out. The same is true of a believer and an unbeliever.

God can draw a straight line with a crooked stick. And in graciousness he has done that in the past for people who have dated and married unbelievers in disobedience. He can convert an unbeliever to a believer and even create a healthy marriage that honors him. But God also draws crooked lines with crooked sticks. And he has done that a lot more often. Best to trust that in the way of what he commands, we will experience what he says can be expected in that way.

Questions/Discussion Points

1. Discuss the following statement: "Dating is not a biblical method of evangelism."

2. How can you be a kind, friendly, and caring witness to an unbeliever of the opposite sex (maybe one you meet at work) without becoming unequally yoked in any way?

Day 18

———

Unity in Doctrine and Life

Read Amos 3:1-8

The Lord God here is convicting Israel of her apostasy. He speaks "against" her in verse one. Though they are still the people he redeemed from Egypt, things are not well. Israel was dismissing the message of the prophets, unconvinced that God had any issue with them as a people. But, does a lion roar when there is no prey? So God's roar through his prophets is not merely noise. Israel must sit up and take heed. Though God commands her to walk with him in the covenant, Israel is taking a different path: one that diverges from him more and more. Their experience is that God is less and less walking with them and is more and more distant. After all, can two walk together except they be agreed?

So too you cannot walk together with your spouse in the experience of one-flesh union, except you are agreed. This agreement starts with a shared new life in Christ as we discussed above. But it also includes how that new life is expressed in accord with God's word. There are many Christians difficult and inadvisable for you to date and marry because of a lack of agreement.

In other words, that the person is a Christian does not *by itself* mean that you should date and marry them.

After all you must *walk* together. The text does not say, Can two live in the same house together, or, Can two be roommates? But it says, "Can two *walk together* except they be agreed?" (v. 3, emphasis added). There is a life you must share with this person *as one flesh*. "Henceforth you go down life's pathway together." When you establish a home together, what doctrinal principles will unite your home? What church will you attend? To what elders will you submit your life? How will you spend your time? How will you raise your children? Of what entertainment will you take part? To what kind of school will you send your children? How will you spend the Lord's day? Will there be family devotions?

As you can see, there is much to be agreed upon if you are going to walk down the pathway of life together. And while some things might seem insignificant to you now, when you start walking down that pathway, principled differences will lead you down divergent paths—pulling two ways on the yoke. This especially becomes true when you raise children together. Two sinful human beings with different personalities have enough sin to battle, but when husband and wife have doctrinal and even serious practical disagreements, it only adds to the pressure on the marriage and home. There are many things to work through in dating. Be agreed with the one you want to marry, thoroughly agreed, *before* you commit to walking down that pathway together.

Questions/Discussion Points

1. Where are the easiest places to find someone with whom you can walk agreed?

2. Do you have to be agreed on everything to be married? How about to start dating? How much, how little? Be specific in your discussion.

3. *[Parents explain something of the amount of work marriage takes due to sin, and the great pressure that would be added on top of that if there was principled disagreement.]*

Day 19

Don't Merely
"Follow Your Heart" but
Follow His Word

Read Deuteronomy 29:29

There will be a lot of talk about "the one." We even pray for "the one" that God has chosen for you. As we discussed before (Day 2), from the point of view of God's decree, there is, of course, only one (if his will for your life is indeed marriage). From that point of view, even if you rebel against everything we are discussing here and you marry "the wrong one," that person is still "the one." God knows and already has determined the one person you will marry.

But God's determination is a secret thing that belongs only to him. You cannot find out who that person is by trying to pry the lid off God's eternal decree. Nor can you find out by simply relying on your feelings or mutual "chemistry." That is the point of today's discussion. We are in a section titled "Principles to Undergird Your Search." Today's starts as a negative one: it isn't as though there is one person out there who so perfectly matches you or makes you feel a certain way that when you find him/her—bingo, that's God revealing his secret will to you about "the one." Feelings are notoriously fickle and can be as unreliable as a magic eight-ball in getting you into the secret will of God.

According to Deuteronomy 29:29 the only way God has given for you (and us as your parents with you) to discover whom to marry is his *revealed* will; that is, his commands and principles for how to date and marry. The things we are talking about in this devotional are his revealed will. Carrying out principles he has revealed can take a lot of wisdom at times, but God's way is not hidden or mysterious. This doesn't mean feelings mean nothing; we'll get to that tomorrow. But our responsibility is to follow what he has revealed. And that's not just true for adults; it's true for us "*and our children*" the text says. And that isn't just true for "way back then," whereas now we have so many great love songs to guide us. The revealed will of God is for us and our children "*forever.*"

It might be tempting at some point to say, "This feeling I have surely is God telling me this person is 'the one,' even if being with this person means I disobey God's word." It might be tempting to say, "Everything just worked out for us to be together, surely God's providence is arranging this, even if his word would say no." God doesn't reveal his secrets to us just by how right something feels or seems. He reveals his secrets to us by his word and by leading us to follow that word.

Questions/Discussion Points

1. What is it about feelings that makes it so tempting to put them above the word of God?

2. Is it possible that what we perceive to be an "open door," is actually a temptation from the evil one?

3. *[Parents, consider sharing with your children a time from your youth when you were tempted to compromise because of strong emotions (this doesn't have to be related to a dating scenario, but could be).]*

Day 20

Set Your Heart on God and Then You May "Follow Your Heart"

Read Psalm 37:1–5

So, if you follow God's revealed will and seek a spouse the way he calls you to, there is not necessarily just one person out there who is "the one" from an earthly point of view. In fact, there might be several who could be "the one." Likely there will be a good number you could marry and with whom you could have a wonderful, delightful, God-glorifying, marriage and home. That's great!

Following the word puts you on the right road. But there can in some instances be a good number of cars on that road. It's here that factors like feelings, emotions, personalities, attraction, and how you "fit" together may rightly come in. Some of these factors are more important than others, but they are all legitimate factors. Psalm 37:4 instructs, "Delight thyself also in the LORD; and he shall give thee the desires of thine heart." If you delight yourself in the Lord, you follow his revealed will. In fact it's impossible to actively delight in the Lord and then flout his revealed will. With your heart thus set ultimately on God and his way, the desires of your heart may come into play.

As one man put it, you climb the mountain of holiness in the Christian life, and you look to see who is climbing with you. Among those who are, you may "follow your heart" to the one whose conversation you enjoy and the one you find attractive. And if he/she regards you the same way then the "fireworks" are a good thing! Don't forget to keep the secondary factors secondary. And remember too that sometimes attraction isn't there right away, but develops over time.

Questions/Discussion Points

1. Committed to the biblical principles for dating and marriage, how important are feelings and attraction when considering a mate? Can we make too much of them even then? Too little?

2. *[Parents, consider taking this opportunity to tell your children about your own "love story." What attracted you first, second to your spouse? You may even consider sharing honestly with your children mistakes you made in your dating and use it to warn your children against disobedience to God and showing God's grace in spite of our sin.]*

Day 21

A Parent's
Responsibility

Read Genesis 24:1–9

It is not the case that when their child becomes a teenager, parents become uninvolved in their child's life. It is not the case either then that when their child becomes a teenager parents have little involvement in their child's dating and marrying. Abraham, as head of the home, knew God gave him a certain responsibility regarding who his child married. His responsibility and authority were God-given. Every father must take the responsibility up, even as Abraham did.

The scriptural teaching is that headship functions like an umbrella. Children and youth are under the umbrella of their father's headship until they establish their own homes. Parental headship is for the protection of children and youth, just as an umbrella protects the person under it from the weather. When a young woman marries, she moves from being under the umbrella of her father, to being under the umbrella of her husband. When a young man gets married, he moves from being under the umbrella of his father, to holding an umbrella over his wife and family. To be sure, when God's will is lifelong singlehood (Day 24), a person establishes a home where they hold the umbrella over themselves. But for our purposes here we stick to illustrating dating and marriage.

Young person, don't kick back against your parents' wise, healthy involvement in your life, including your dating life. Even though we just discussed the place of emotions in Days 19 and 20, it may be that you don't see things so clearly when you are in the situation. Don't kick back against the helpful evaluations of others in your family and church either. Returning to the story of Abraham, notice that more than the parents are involved here. There is also Eliezer, and there is Laban, Rebekah's brother, too. The point is, when you seek a mate, welcome the healthy involvement of your family in your dating and marriage, and those with whom you are close in the covenant community.

This doesn't mean *you won't* be involved, of course. Neither does it mean that *your* own thoughts and feelings on the matter have no importance. At the end of the day Rebekah's family still, "called Rebekah, and said unto her, Wilt thou go with this man? And she said, I will go" (Gen. 24:58). This interplay between the family and the young person will look different depending on the family and the young person and his/her age perhaps, but it must be there. Maybe you noticed the word "healthy" a couple of times above. There can be too much involvement. But the temptation for most homes is too *little*, not too *much*.

May the Lord grant that through this process, if the day comes that you do get married, your family and covenant community around you respond this way: "And it came to pass, that, when Abraham's servant heard their words, he worshipped the LORD, bowing himself to the earth" (v. 52). And, "Then Laban and Bethuel answered and said, The thing proceedeth from the LORD!" (v. 50).

Questions/Discussion Points

1. Who must give the final approval for whom you date and whom you marry?

2. Does it sound uncomfortable to talk openly with your parents about your dating life? Why or why not? How can we make it more comfortable?

Day 22

———

Parental Challenge
and Approval

Read Joshua 14:6–14; Joshua 15:13–17

Perhaps you are thinking "I've got this dating thing on my own." But you do need help, even beyond our discussions this month. As we learned last time, God has ordained that parents are involved in this process—they help, guide, oversee, and finally approve or disapprove who their children date and marry.

God has ordained that the buck stop specifically with the father who is head of his home. A good, open relationship with your father (and mother) will go a long way. Also, not getting mad when dad and mom give biblical requirements for anyone who will date you, and when they check to see if the person you are interested in matches those requirements.

In today's reading we see that Caleb had requirements for whoever would marry his daughter, and he held to those requirements when the time came. They boil down to three—total trust in the word of God, a life of putting faith into action, and an application of that way of living to the man's life with his daughter.

Caleb was one of the two faithful spies. He had been to Canaan before. God had promised faithful Caleb that he would receive whatever portion of the land he wanted once the Israelites got into Canaan (Josh. 14:9). Throughout his life, Caleb trusted the promises of God, even when the rest of Israel did not (Num. 13:30). Now he trusts that God would give *this* portion to *his* family specifically, even though he was 85 years old and would have to fight literal giants to get it! In fact, *this is why* Caleb wanted *this part* of the land specifically. He wanted to show God would give it to him as promised, though it was inhabited by giants and he would be wielding a sword at 85 years old (Josh. 14:12).

Caleb wanted a man for his daughter who trusted the word of God as he did. There were many in Israel who did not. Caleb made total, firm, unshaken faith in everything God had said a requirement. Caleb wasn't just looking for talk, but talk that was confirmed in the walk. So, Caleb set up a trust-fall requirement. A trust-fall is where someone closes their eyes and lets their body fall backward, trusting that the waiting arms behind them will catch them. The man for Caleb's daughter must show his faith in God's promises by staking his life on them: come fight giants with me!

Good fathers and mothers will do similarly. They will examine the confession and life of someone you want to date. They will look for him/her to *show* they are in bud form the kind of person we talked about in Days 8–16. Is this person willing to stand alone upon God's word in faith when the pressure comes? Is this person willing to do the hard thing, in order to remain grounded upon God's truth? Is this person willing to face giant enemies of God and his truth, and giant enemies in his/her own personal faith and walk? Is this person applying faith to the relationship they have with our son or daughter? Your parents have to know, ask, walk with the person you are interested in to find out. It's their job. Yes, they have to be careful how they do it, and they have to battle idealism too sometimes. But it's their job out of love for God and you. It is *them* putting faith in God's word into action!

Questions/Discussion Points

1. *[Parents, share your own opinions and ask for your children's thoughts.]* What do you think about the old practice of Dad first interviewing the person who wants to date you or whom you want to date?

2. *[Parents, share your own opinions and ask for your children's thoughts.]* How can we as parents get to know the person you want to date or are now dating in a way that is helpful and comfortable, yet faithful to the responsibility God gives us?

Beware of Dangers

Day 23

Blinding Lust

Read 2 Samuel 13:1–5; 1 Peter 5:8; 2 Corinthians 2:11

Now obviously if you had been there you would have said to Amnon, "It's not love Amnon, it's lust! Desire has overcome your ability to judge—it's clouding your mind, and it's leading you into terrible, terrible sin!" But what if you meet someone at work, a boy/girl who is so handsome/beautiful? And he/she keeps talking to you and making you laugh, and your shifts keep lining up, and everyone else who works there is starting to talk about how good you would be together, and there is even a coworker named Jonadab who has said he is willing to close for you tonight so you can go hang out with that co-worker? Oh, and you know just as well as your parents that this is not someone you should be dating…What will you do?

As we move into this new section on dangers to beware of, the first is that hormonal changes that have happened/are happening/will happen in you, may tempt you in the moment to let go of everything we've talked about, and everything correct you can say about Amnon right now. There is a great temptation to mistake lust for love. And that temptation becomes even more powerful when you are under the influence of music, movies, books, co-workers, and friends, who sing and talk and love as though lust and love are the same. The combination of your own depraved old man, hormonal changes that are preparing you for marriage, and the message of the world, will tempt you to imagine the possibilities. And what used to be standards and boundaries, are now the remains of the Great Wall of China— merely a reminder of what once was.

"Be sober, be vigilant; because your adversary the devil, as a roaring lion, walketh about, seeking whom he may devour" (1 Pet. 5:8). Read twice the following warning from C. S. Lewis in letter twenty-six of *The Screwtape Letters*. Remember, this is a fictional demon giving advice to another fictional demon about how to tempt young people.

> Yes, courtship [dating] is the time for sowing those seeds which will grow up ten years later into domestic hatred. The enchantment of unsatisfied desire produces results which the humans can be made to mistake for the results of [biblical] charity. Avail yourself of the ambiguity in the word "Love": let them think they have solved by Love problems they have in fact only waived or postponed under the influence of the enchantment. While it lasts you have your chance to foment the problems in secret and render them chronic.*

[If age appropriate] Even more, if you give in to sexual temptation, and not even "all the way," the devil will have such a strong hold on you. There will be "strong delusion," (2 Thess. 2:11). The

---

* C. S. Lewis, *The Screwtape Letters and Screwtape Proposes a Toast*, (New York: Time Inc., 1963), 92.

call of scripture is urgent, "That every one of you should know how to possess his vessel in sanctification and honour; not in the lust of concupiscence, even as the Gentiles which know not God" (1 Thess. 4:4-5). How many of God's children have entered relationships and even marriages they knew they never should have entered into because they bowed to the god of lust and assumed it would all work out in the end. How many have families like David's, with Amnons and Absaloms as a consequence! Proverbs 6:27, "Can a man take fire in his bosom, and his clothes not be burned?" Be oh so careful, lest Satan should get an advantage of us: for we are not ignorant of his devices!

Questions/Discussion Points

1. What is true love?

2. *[If age appropriate]* Why is reserving the God-given gift of sex for marriage so important as you go through the process of looking for a spouse?

3. Give an example of a time when your judgments have been clouded by your desires. How easily do you think your judgment can be clouded like Amnon's?

Day 24

Making an Idol
Out of Marriage

Read Isaiah 56:1–7

The first danger you must beware of as you search for a husband or wife is blinding lust that would tempt you to be with the wrong person in the wrong way or even the right person in the wrong way. The second danger (that we cover today) is a blinding desire *for marriage itself* that would tempt you to be willing to be with the wrong kind of person. The danger here is that you would be so in love with the *idea* of marriage, or the *idea* of having children, that you are unwilling to remain single until God brings you the right kind of person (even if that means your whole life). This is a danger that would lead you to say, "I will compromise; I just want to be married."

This is a real danger, especially if it is God's will that you get a bit older and see many of your friends marry, yet you remain single yourself. There have been those who have gone before you, discontent with singlehood, who have been willing to give up marrying *in the Lord* just to have *marriage*.

You ought to at least reckon with the possibility that singlehood may be God's will for you. It's true, the general way of things in God's covenant is that we marry in the Lord and have a family. But there are times when God says no to that. Or times when God says, "not when everybody else is getting this, but much later." Or times when God says, "I will give you a spouse, but I will not give you children." Marriage and a family are not things God promises to us individually.

One of the things that will help fight off the temptation to idolize marriage and children is seeing that singlehood is itself a good gift of God. The passage we read today helps here. The passage is telling us that God's "house shall be called an house of prayer for all people" (v. 7). Specifically, in the text, "all people" includes the "stranger" (the convert not born and raised in a Christian home), and the "eunuch" (a single member of the church, or one married but childless). These are members who are tempted to say (v. 3), "The LORD hath utterly separated me from his people!" (I am different from everyone and thus separate from them). Or, (v. 3), "Behold I am a dry tree" (I am not fruitful because I don't have any children like most others here in the church)! Lacking spouses and/or children, these church members are tempted to think they are not as important to God as others, that they are "economy class" Christians compared to the "first class" Christians born in the church, or with spouses and children.

In the text God gives three reasons why these tempting thoughts are false.

1. These may "take hold of my covenant" as much as anyone else (v. 4). In fact, speaking of the single or childless, these are often able to take hold of God's covenant in a way that married members or those with children cannot! God's covenant at its heart is a relationship of fellowship with God. Often the single

or childless are closer to God because He is their dearest friend.

2. "Unto them will I give...a name better than of sons and daughters: I will give them an everlasting name, that shall not be cut off" (v. 5). Single or childless members don't have sons and daughters to carry on their earthly last name. But God says he will give them a name better than any earthly name. That is, the name of son or daughter *of God!* That's an everlasting name that will never be cut off.

3. I "make them joyful in my house of prayer" (v. 7). That is, I give them joy in serving me in my church. This is the same thing Paul speaks of in 1 Corinthians 7:32 when he says singlehood gives the privilege of more time to care "for the things that belong to the Lord." God gives single and childless Christians joyful lives given over to the service of God and others without the responsibility of marriage or children.

Knowing this about singlehood, you are less tempted to pursue marriage "at all costs." A single life in the church is a blessed and good life. Marriage and children may not hold a place in your life reserved for God alone. Your source of happiness is that you know him, whatever his will is for you.

Questions/Discussion Points

1. Are there any single members of the church you know who are a good example of obedience, contentment, and joy with God's way with them even though they would say they desire marriage?

2. How could a person sinfully idolize marriage and children, even if God *does* give them a right marriage, and children too?

3. Discuss this statement: The more your relationship with God grows the more content (and joyful!) you will be whether single or married.

—

False Faith

Read Joshua 9:1–16

We have looked at two dangers so far, blinding lust, and making an idol out of marriage. A third is the danger of false commitment. God had commanded the Israelites to make no treaty with the inhabitants of the land once God brought them to Canaan. Instead they were to eradicate the people there, all of whom had filled the cup of iniquity (Deut. 7:1–2; 20:16–18). The Gibeonites, aware that they stood no chance against this God-anointed band, tried a different approach from the other "ites" in the area: find a way to bind themselves to Israel in matrimony. But how to accomplish that when the Father (God) had told his daughter (Israel) not to date any of the ungodly in the land? The only way to "get the girl" was to pretend to be something they were not. It wouldn't necessarily matter if the Father could see through it, as long as the daughter couldn't. All they needed was enough time to win her heart.

This has played out before with earthly fathers and their earthly daughters. Sadly, it will happen again, not only with daughters but sons too. Emotions can be so powerful. They not only can make a person want to believe someone genuinely has a heart after God, they can even make the *other person* want to pretend *to have* a heart after God. The Gibeonites not only pretended to be from far enough away to not come under God's command for eradication, they pretended to reverence the same God the daughter reverenced (Josh. 9:9-11). Sometimes a person may be deliberately deceptive, knowing they just need to play the game long enough until they can steal her away. Other times, a person may not even be fully conscious of the fact that it is the girl/boy—not the God—that they "love." When the strong emotions fade after a year or two of marriage, the common faith upon which a marriage must be built is not there, and the devastating truth comes out (v. 16).

Part of the problem was that Joshua moved too quickly (vv. 14-15). He naively believed the confession of the Gibeonites. He did not proceed slowly, with caution, to judge if the story and confession was genuine. Let that be a lesson. Time will generally tell. Don't date someone without a *history* of confession and life of genuine service to God and the faith. In addition, Joshua did not lay the matter before the Lord (v. 14). How important that we pray and seek God's word on the matter, reminding ourselves what genuine faith and its effects look like.

There are still Gibeonite boys and Gibeonite girls out there, some of whom have grown up in the church all their life, others who have feigned conversion. They leave a wake of devastation behind them for generations, even in the lives of faithful children of God. We may not be cynical either, of course. Tomorrow's lesson will help with that. But this danger is real. May God give us wisdom to avoid it.

Questions/Discussion Points

1. *[Parents, do you know of any cases of this with which to warn your children? (withholding names if necessary, of course).]*

2. If the devil hates godly marriages, do you think he might try to send a Gibeonite or two into your life at some point?

Judging Others for Their Background and Not God's Work in Them

Read Joshua 2:8-13; 6:22-25

There is a dangerous ditch opposite the one we discussed in yesterday's lesson. That danger is dismissing God's genuine work in someone's life despite their background or family situation. Here we are applying the passage not only to people who were not raised in a faithful home and church, but also to those who have been born into the sphere of the covenant and have rebelled for a time.

The last thing the spies would have expected was to find a former prostitute in Jericho confessing faith in Jehovah! Who would have thought that Rahab would be listed in the hall of faith in Hebrews 11, and, even more astoundingly, listed in the genealogy of Christ himself as one of his grandmothers? God can and does work despite a person's background. He is the sovereign Lord of heaven and earth, and of the hearts and lives of people too.

It is interesting to compare Rahab's confession to the confession of the Gibeonites from yesterday's devotion. The Gibeonites say, "From a very far country thy servants are come because of the name of the Lord thy God: for we have heard the fame of him, and all that he did in Egypt, and all that he did to the two kings of the Amorites, that *were* beyond Jordan, to Sihon king of Heshbon, and to Og king of Bashan, which *was* at Ashtaroth" (Josh. 9:9–10, emphasis added). Rahab says, "For we have heard how the Lord dried up the water of the Red sea for you, when ye came out of Egypt; and what ye did unto the two kings of the Amorites, that *were* on the other side Jordan, Sihon and Og, whom ye utterly destroyed" (Josh. 2:10). They are virtually the same. So how do you know who is genuine and who is not?

What the Gibeonites and Rahab say are not *exactly* the same. Rahab adds this, "for the Lord your God, he *is* God in heaven above, and in earth beneath" (Josh. 2:11). A more personal and urgent confession (like what Moses calls Israel to confess in Deut. 4:39). However, the main difference is that over time, and in difficult circumstances, Rahab showed her faith by her works (James 2:25). First, she was willing to cut off her former way of life utterly and completely, holding nothing back. She forsook her past life and even her past friends for the sake of her confession. And she did so at the risk of her life. If a soldier would have rustled around in the flax with his spear and discovered the spies there, she would have been killed. Second, she not only negatively forsook the world, but positively consecrated herself to God and his kingdom. She tied the scarlet cord to her window in faith. And, Joshua 6:25 tells us, "Joshua saved Rahab the harlot alive, and her father's household, and all that she had; *and she dwelleth in Israel even unto this day*" (emphasis added). She proved her faith over a length of time, joining with the people of God, learning the works and ways of Jehovah, worshipping with God's people, and entering into the life of God's covenant willingly and actively.

Matthew 1:5 tells us that eventually Rahab married an Israelite named Salmon. Jewish tradition has it that he was one of the two spies. But notice, he did not put a ring on her finger after his conversation with her that day upon the wall. He didn't pursue her until after she had shown herself a genuine part of the people of God in her heart and life for a lengthy period of time. Joshua committed way too early. Salmon waited and watched the Lord sovereignly work.

Questions/Discussion Points

1. How do the doctrines of grace (the five points of Calvinism) lead us to believe God can perform works today like he performed in Rahab, both in those outside the church, and those inside who have lived in rebellion for a time?

2. Given this devotion and the previous one, how can you discern the difference (never infallibly) between someone who loves the Reformed faith, and one who is only going through the motions? How do you not distrust the Lord's genuine work, but at the same time not be naïve?

3. With today's devotion in mind, explain the importance of observing the person you are dating (or desire to date) while he/she engages in "normal life" apart from the fun and leisure of a date.

A Mysterious Joy

Day 27: The Way of a Man with a Maid

Day 27

The Way of a Man
with a Maid

Read Proverbs 30:18-20

The Holy Spirit speaks of four things that, though explainable in many respects, in the end give way to mystery. In other words, things that force one to finally stop trying to explain how it all works, so that he can instead stand back and watch in delight with awe and wonder at God's design. The first thing the Spirit notes is watching an eagle fly; how it defies gravity and moves so fluidly between graceful floating and beating the air for speed. The second observation is of the way a serpent moves upon a rock; how without legs it glides across the surface. The third is the way a ship moves across the sea; how such a heavy object floats across the water. You can get out your science book and explain these things scientifically. But even after you do that, you still should be able to appreciate the wonder of it. There is something about it, even after you do the math, that is beyond you.

The fourth example given is the way of a man with a maid. The word "maid" is the word for virgin. The Spirit is talking about the wonder of a man and woman who are romantically inclined to each other, who approach marriage, and finally get married and consummate their marriage. He is talking about two who are doing so in godliness and purity, according to the way of God's word. That's why the next verse speaks of the opposite: an adulteress who engages in her conquests and feels no sting of conscience, but merely satisfies desires like eating a meal. "Such is the way of an adulteress woman, she eateth and wipeth her mouth" (v. 20). A wonder-less sight.

One of the tragedies of sin having power over dating and marriage is that there is no God-glorifying mystery and wonder to it all! Instead there is only the crass satisfying of cravings, no different than scarfing down a burger and moving on! But the selfless dance of two in Christ discovering one another as creations of God, resisting self to seek and serve the other, even as such selflessness plays on one another to increase the desire and bond—that is a wonder beyond telling!

There is in the process of dating and engagement the feeling of being drawn to each other, the wanting to spend hours talking, the inside jokes and laughter, the attraction that builds, the loving just to spend time together even if what you are doing isn't that exciting. There is the growing way two begin to read each other's thoughts by the look on the face, the way two lives progressively melt into each other. It is a wonderful mystery and should be. Even as the future husband and wife in Song of Solomon are committed to the law of God for their purity—"stir not up, nor awaken my love, until he please" (8:4)—the wonder, romance, and mystery is palpable all the way through. "Let him kiss me with the kisses of his mouth: for thy love is better than wine" (1:2). This should be in a relationship. It should be something that two can even look back upon in tough times and draw from with joy (5:17).

[This paragraph if age appropriate] Think of the way godly trust and desire have been built up in the relationship that honors God.

Then comes the time when this trust may properly be expressed in the intimacy of sex in marriage. As the woman opens herself up to this man with a vulnerability that she has not known before, she does so precisely because he has earned that trust in his selfless devotion and commitment. On the man's part, there is the "taking" of his wife, with a powerful yet protecting love. This too speaks of Christ and his church. The intimacy of Christ and his bride is a mystery (Eph. 5:32). Why would we expect that what reflects it would lack wonder and awe? In the confines of a scriptural relationship, the mystery is a holy and glorious thing. And the wonder of it is another reason to date and marry in the biblical way.

It is marvelous that when scripture describes dating and marriage before the face of God, it doesn't stop with giving authoritative guidelines. It also allows for mystery and wonder and commends it. Everything discussed in this devotional is misused if it makes a relationship calculated, mathematical, and leaves it without any awe. There are guidelines—scriptural guidelines, authoritative guidelines—and they must be honored as such. But within their borders, there ought to be a certain joy and wonder and mystery and freedom that is like breathing in mountain air from the top of a grand peak. The Holy Spirit wrote Song of Solomon too.

Questions/Discussion Points

1. Is it wise to keep progressing in a relationship where this mystery is absent? Is this a deal-breaker? Is there a sliding scale we can wisely appreciate?

2. What do you do, if you have mysterious attraction, but parents and others are pointing out to you that it is outside scriptural bounds? Is it beautiful in God's sight?

An Example to Emulate

Ruth in Ruth 1

Don't underestimate the power of a good example. Some people, by grace, can set a good example for others without seeing a good example themselves (Ruth). Others have a hard time setting a good example without having one to follow themselves (the vast majority of us). Hopefully your parents can recount their dating life as a good example to you, and hopefully their marriage is a good example to you now. But in God's sovereign wisdom maybe one or both is not. And of course, this side of heaven, any example, even a good one, is going to be marred with sin and failure. Boaz and Ruth were sinners too, and their example was tainted with sin and failure. Nonetheless, scripture sets up Boaz and Ruth as a wonderful example of two godly people pursuing marriage.

As such, their example is worth examining, praying over, and remembering. The devil uses the world to promote a God-forsaken view of love, sex, dating, marriage, and family. The dangerous message comes to us through music, text, images, and even real life people. But the word in the hands of the Spirit can hold this tidal wave back. Let us add this final piece to what we have seen in scripture, a scriptural *example* from real life people. We are going to take a chapter a day out of the book of Ruth. The

challenge will be to point out things about Ruth and Boaz that
are good examples of what we have studied.

> *[Begin each of the next four devotions by reading the
> chapter for the day, letting everyone know we are silently
> watching for a godly example in Ruth and Boaz as we read.
> Then go back through that chapter again and together
> point out what good examples can be found. Below, you
> will see under each day's reading, a list of things that I and
> my family found for each chapter that make Ruth and Boaz
> a good example. This will be like a "cheat sheet" for you.
> But hopefully you can find the same on your own, and even
> add other observations. If you want to go the extra mile,
> see if you can connect some of what you find in Ruth and
> Boaz to specific devotions from previous days. After you
> are finished with each day's devotion, pray together for the
> children and youth of the home that this example would be
> what they look up to instead of the examples in the world.]*

Read Ruth 1, and then go back and find at least these things about Ruth's godliness:

- Verses 1-6—In spite of the bad example in the family
  she married into, Ruth is committed to the Lord.

- Verses 11-13—Ruth is willing to give up the potential
  of husband and children to live single for the sake of
  God and his people. Her relationship with God was
  more important.

- Verse 14-15—Ruth's confession is tried and comes
  forth as gold. Ruth cleaves to Naomi despite being
  told to go back and find a husband of Moab (vv.
  8-13). This shows her commitment to the Lord.

- Verse 14-15—Ruth cleaves to Naomi, even when Orpah leaves and goes back. Ruth does not merely follow peer pressure.

- Verse 15—The gods of Ruth's culture do not have a hold on her.

- Verses 16-17—Ruth's confession is total and whole-hearted.

Ruth and Boaz in Ruth 2

Read Ruth 2, and then go back and find at least these things about the godliness of Ruth and Boaz and their initial meeting:

Ruth

- Verse 2—Ruth voluntarily cares about needs and is willing to fill them.

- Verse 10—Ruth is humble, respectful, and thankful. She is not spoiled and expecting attention.

- Verse 11—Ruth's life left no doubt about her confession and godliness. Ruth's reputation was based on her confession and life. Boaz notices. Live godly and the right kind of person will notice.

- Verse 13—Again, Ruth is humble, not proud and expecting extra attention.

- Verse 17—Ruth is a hard worker, working till sundown.

Boaz

- Verse 4—Boaz is not merely a "Sunday Christian." He takes his faith to work with him and makes it a part of his regular life.

- Verse 5—Boaz is on the lookout for those who have needs.

- Verses 8-9, 14-16—Boaz uses his money to care for the needy and vulnerable and is unhesitatingly generous to the same.

- Verse 9—Boaz wants to protect women, not take advantage of them. (This is the time of the Judges, young men were not always trustworthy).

- Verse 11—Godliness strikes Boaz more than any other characteristic. His eye and ear is tuned to a commitment to God and the church and one's family.

- Verse 14—Though he has money, Boaz is not arrogant and snooty. He enjoys fellowship with those of lesser status than himself.

- Verses 21-23—Boaz' care for others is not merely "one and done." His care is a consistent and committed part of his character (until the end of barley and wheat harvest).

Ruth and Boaz
in Ruth 3

Read Ruth 3, and then go back and find at least these things about the romance of Ruth and Boaz:

Ruth

- Verse 3—Feminine beauty and appeal is not a bad thing in itself.

- Verses 5-6—Ruth is obedient to her mother. She heeds wise parental advice.

- Verse 10—Ruth is looking for godliness first, not external things like youth or money.

- Verse 11—Ruth is a virtuous woman and has a reputation as such.

Boaz

- Verse 7—Boaz himself works hard. He doesn't just let his men do all the work while he is lazy.

- Verse 10—Boaz is humble.

- Verse 11—Boaz wanted to keep a good reputation. He cared about the church's opinion of him.

- Verses 12-13—Boaz obeyed God's law even though it went against the grain of what he desired. How important for all aspects of dating!

- Verse 14—Boaz cared not only for his own reputation among God's people, but for Ruth's as well.

- Verse 15—Boaz cared about the *family* of the one he cared about.

- Verse 18—Boaz' character was known. He had a reputation for seeing things through.

Day 31

Boaz in Ruth 4

Read Ruth 4, and then go back and find at least these things about Boaz' leadership:

- Verses 1-2—Boaz is willing to lead.

- Verses 1-5—Boaz sticks to his convictions to honor God's law; he doesn't sway from his earlier conviction.

- Verse 9—Boaz honors the authority of the elders of the church.

- Verse 10 in contrast to verse 6—Boaz' love is self-less and sacrificial. He would protect the name of Ruth's dead husband and father-in-law, possibly at the expense of carrying on his own name.

- Verse 22—God blesses Boaz and Ruth's faithfulness. They had no idea they would be a part of the line of Christ. They are simply faithful, trusting God will take care of the results.

Conclusion

You made it! Now that you as a family have finished this 31-day devotional, my prayer is that the youth have seen the wonder of marriage, been convicted of the biblical manner of pursuing marriage, and been encouraged to pursue the kind of relationship with God that prepares them for this honorable state. Perhaps going through it with their youth has even helped parents grow in their marriages! My prayer is that this devotional book would be used by God as a tool to provide the church with another generation of healthy and godly marriages and homes. The Lord's blessings as you pursue marriage to his glory!

In Christian love,

Rev. Cory Griess

CPSIA information can be obtained
at www.ICGtesting.com
Printed in the USA
FSHW022333100122
87489FS